Searching for Cures

by Melissa McDaniel

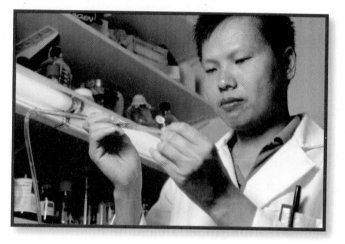

Table of Contents

Introduction

Why do people get sick? What causes disease? Many ancient peoples believed that evil spirits caused sickness or that disease was punishment from angry gods.

People once had murky ideas about disease and its cause. Illness was commonly treated through magic and religion. Some cultures used special plants to heal the sick. The bark of the willow tree has been successfully used to treat pain for thousands of years. But even when these herbs helped, no one understood why. The actual cause of disease remained a mystery.

⌒ Draining blood was a common cure for many centuries.

Over time people began studying disease with science. They looked through microscopes and were able to see the tiny organisms that cause illnesses to erupt. Their discoveries explained how diseases spread. This finally allowed cures to be developed.

Medical research has come a long way. Modern medicine has saved millions of lives. But researchers continue to search for cures to battle new diseases.

Medical researchers are
always looking for new and
better cures for diseases.

CHAPTER ONE

Discovering Microbes

You probably know that hearts pump blood and muscles move bones. But basic ideas of human biology like these were unknown for most of history. Centuries ago there were laws against cutting open bodies. Few had seen inside a human body. How could people understand what they couldn't see?

This began to change in the 1300s. Great thinkers in Europe became interested in science—and medicine. Cutting open a dead person to study it hadn't been allowed. But now laws against human **dissection** were relaxed. Scientists could finally study the body in detail. Leonardo da Vinci made some 750 drawings from dissections. These early scientists learned how the human body is put together.

The artist ➲ and scientist Leonardo da Vinci lived in the 1400s. He was a careful observer and studied human anatomy to learn how the body worked.

People have been using microscopes ➲ to look at microbes for more than 400 years. This microscope is from the 1600s.

A Closer Look

Early scientists didn't just want to understand how the body works. They also wanted to solve the mystery of disease. An invention first created around 1600 became their most important tool. It was the microscope.

The first microscopes worked much like modern ones do today. First a **specimen** is put on a piece of glass. Then a person looks down through a tube. Fitted inside the tube are lenses. The lenses magnify the specimen, making it appear larger.

Microscopes started scientists down the right path. They helped them discover what causes disease. In 1674 a Dutch scientist put a drop of water under a microscope. Antoni van Leeuwenhoek (AHN-tohnee vahn LAY-vun-HOOK) was amazed! He observed many "little animals" in the water. These kinds of microscopic organisms are called **microbes**.

Leeuwenhoek was the first person to see microbes. But he didn't make the connection between microbes and disease. It would take another two centuries for someone to figure that out.

In 1864 Louis Pasteur was studying why wine turns sour. The French chemist believed that **bacteria** spoiled the wine. When Pasteur heated new wine, the bacteria were killed and the wine didn't spoil. Pasteur was the first to link rotting food to living microbes. Until then most people believed that food spoiled because of a chemical reaction. Pasteur's research led the chemist to believe that bacteria also cause diseases.

Pasteurization

Louis Pasteur suspected that bacteria caused milk, like wine, to sour. He decided to prove it. He heated the milk to a high temperature to kill the bacteria. This made the milk safe and helped keep it from spoiling. This heating process is called pasteurization.

↻ French chemist Louis Pasteur lived from 1822–1895. He was the first person to link microbes with disease.

This is pneumonia ➲
bacteria magnified
thousands of times.
Pneumonia is an
infection of
the lungs.

Germ Theory

What Louis Pasteur had discovered is called the germ theory of disease. Harmful microbes, or germs, get into your body and multiply. This invasion of microbes is what makes you sick.

Soon a German doctor made another important discovery. Robert Koch proved that the serious disease called anthrax comes from particular rod-shaped bacteria. Koch discovered that different bacteria cause different diseases.

By the end of the 1900s, researchers had found harmful bacteria that cause many diseases. Soon other scientists discovered another kind of microbe, one that also causes disease. It is called a **virus**. Viruses only live inside other **cells**. They are very small and simple microbes. But viruses cause many of our worst and most common diseases. AIDS, chickenpox, and measles all come from viruses.

CHAPTER TWO

Fighting Disease

Microbes like bacteria and viruses are everywhere. Many are harmless. Those that cause disease are called germs, or **pathogens**. Some kinds of pathogens thrive in water. Unclean water sickens many people. Food-borne pathogens such as salmonella bacteria are why it's important to cook eggs and meat well and quickly refrigerate leftovers.

Other germs travel through the air, like the flu and cold viruses. You can breathe them in or pick them up.

Insects are another way pathogens are passed along. Lyme disease is spread through tick bites. Mosquitoes can carry the West Nile virus.

Typhoid Mary

A person who is infected with a disease but isn't sick is called a carrier. The most famous example was a cook named Mary Mallon. Mallon carried the pathogen for typhoid fever. She spread the disease to more than 50 people without being sick herself. She became known as Typhoid Mary.

Killing Bacteria

By the early 1900s scientists knew that bacteria caused diseases. Now they had to find a way to kill bacteria and cure those diseases.

↻ When Alexander Fleming was presented with the Nobel Prize in medicine in 1945, he said, "Nature makes penicillin, I just found it."

A Scottish scientist named Alexander Fleming took up the challenge. One day in 1928 he saw something odd. It was in one of the dishes where he grew bacteria for experiments. There was **mold** growing in it. But Fleming didn't just throw it out. Instead he took a closer look. He noticed that the bacteria around the mold were dead. Fleming had discovered the bacteria-killing mold, **penicillin**. Penicillin mold was later made into a powerful medicine.

Discovering penicillin was a lucky accident. Penicillin became a drug that kills bacteria. It was the first **antibiotic**. Antibiotics cure diseases from strep throat to scarlet fever.

Antibiotics don't cure all diseases. Taking antibiotics doesn't help the common cold. Viruses cause colds and the flu. Finding drugs to battle viruses is a newer science. Most antiviral drugs don't completely cure a disease. They just make it less serious. Creating antivirals is complicated. Viruses only live inside other cells. Scientists are learning more about viruses and working on new antiviral drugs.

⟳ Doctors first used penicillin in 1941. During World War II (1939–1945), penicillin saved many wounded soldiers by curing their infections.

The Immune System

Fortunately, there are other ways to fight diseases besides drugs. The body itself does a lot of the work. Our **immune system** is built to battle disease. Special blood cells seek out pathogens and destroy them.

The immune system defends itself best with familiar germs. Seek-and-destroy cells work better and more quickly if they've encountered the germs before. **Vaccines** put this fact to work. Vaccines create immunity to a certain disease. When you get vaccinated, a weakened form of the disease is put into your body. This teaches your immune system to recognize this disease. Then you're ready to fight off the disease if you're later exposed to it.

⊙ These cells have been dyed pink to make them easier to see under a microscope.

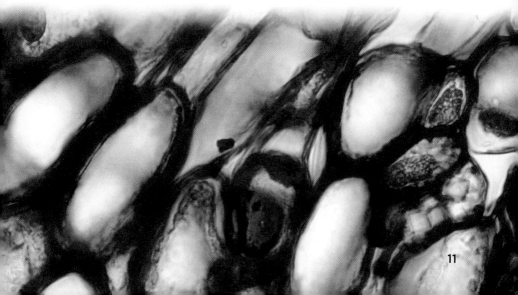

CHAPTER THREE

Preventing Disease

Vaccines are one way to prevent diseases. They keep millions of people around the world healthy.

Humans used vaccines long before they understood the immune system. Smallpox was a serious disease. It can kill and covers people in sores, or pox. Smallpox can cause blindness, too. In ancient China some people were given small amounts of smallpox germs on purpose. Healers ground up scabs from smallpox sufferers. Then they put this powder in the nose of someone who'd never had smallpox. This crude vaccine created smallpox immunity in some. But unfortunately, it gave others the deadly disease.

⟳ More than 100 million children are vaccinated around the world each year.

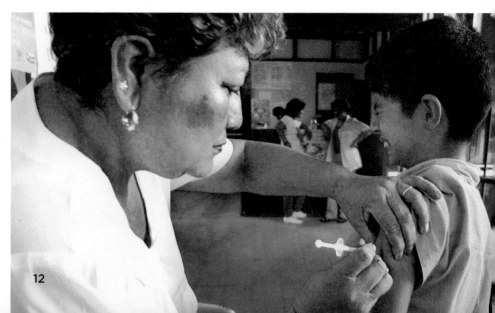

Spreading Diseases

European settlers to the Americas brought more than horses, cattle, pigs, and seeds with them. They carried many diseases that Native Americans had never been exposed to before. The Europeans had thousands of years of built-up immunity to these diseases. Diseases such as smallpox and measles killed millions of Native American, many more than died in wars with the Europeans.

Stamping Out Smallpox

In the late 1700s, Edward Jenner noticed something curious. Milkmaids who got a mild disease called cowpox never got smallpox. It gave the English doctor an idea. In 1796, Jenner took some liquid from a sore on a milkmaid's hand. Next he put the cowpox liquid on the cut arm skin of an 8-year-old boy. Six weeks later the boy was exposed to smallpox. Jenner's vaccine worked. The boy never got smallpox.

Some 100,000 people were vaccinated by 1900. Smallpox remains only in labs today. It's one disease that has been entirely wiped out worldwide.

⋒ Edward Jenner created the word *vaccine*. It comes from the Latin word for cow, "vaca."

Quest for Vaccines

As doctors and scientists learned more about diseases, they started to develop other vaccines. In 1885 Louis Pasteur created a vaccine for rabies. Rabies is usually spread through animal bites.

Polio was one of the most feared diseases of the 1900s. Outbreaks of the crippling disease during the 1940s and 1950s worried parents. They kept their children away from movie theaters, swimming pools, and other crowded places. Polio left millions of children unable to walk.

Jonas Salk, developed the polio vaccine in 1954. The American researcher tested the vaccine on his own family! Vaccines now protect people around the world. They save lives from many diseases.

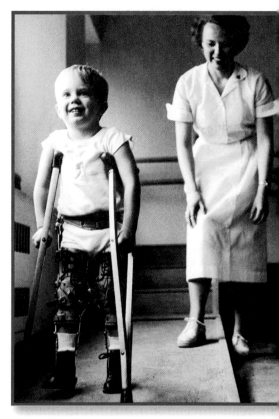

During the 1950s, ↺ more than 20,000 people came down with polio in the United States each year.

CHAPTER FOUR

Outbreak

Medical research has produced cures, vaccines, or treatments for many diseases. But new diseases keep appearing. One of the most fearsome is Ebola. This deadly virus causes fever, headache, and severe bleeding inside the body. Most people who get Ebola die from it. It is 80 to 90 percent fatal.

The Ebola virus is transferred through touching infected blood or other body fluids. Chimpanzees can also be infected with the disease. Handling sick or dead chimpanzees is another way the disease is spread.

Medical workers ⊃ need to wear special protective clothing when treating Ebola patients.

New Tools

Scientists are constantly searching for new and better tools to use in the fight against disease. One important invention was the electron microscope. These microscopes were first made in the 1940s and are far more powerful than regular microscopes.

Electron microscopes can magnify things, like the red blood cells shown here, more than a million times. Electron microscopes allow scientists to see inside viruses.

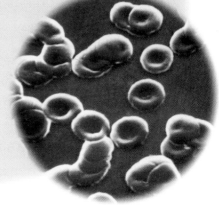

When researchers hear about an Ebola outbreak, they take fast action. First they try to stop the disease from spreading. Patients are isolated, and medical workers wear protective clothing. Then researchers try to learn everything about the disease. They study who had it first and where exactly that person had been. Doctors keep track of symptoms and how well any treatments work.

These studies help treat future victims and may eventually lead to a cure. But it can take a long time. So far, scientists have not come up with drugs or vaccines effective against Ebola.

Ebola is a deadly disease. But outbreaks have been small so far and all have occurred in Central Africa. About 1,300 people have died from Ebola since it was first identified in 1976.

The AIDS Crisis

Diseases newer than Ebola have spread faster and farther. Doctors first noticed AIDS in the early 1980s. In the past twenty-five years AIDS has killed more than 25 million people. AIDS is now a **pandemic**. More than 38 million people around the world carry HIV. HIV is the virus that causes AIDS.

Researchers hope to someday create a vaccine against HIV. But so far their work hasn't succeeded. HIV attacks the body's own immune system and kills cells that fight off disease. AIDS was once a fatal disease. However, today HIV-infected people can control the disease by taking several different drugs.

↻ Researchers still hope to find a cure for AIDS and a vaccine against HIV.

Fighting Malaria

New diseases aren't the only troublesome ones. Malaria has been around for centuries. It's caused by a parasite passed through mosquito bites. Malaria is usually curable. But the disease still kills about two million people a year. Most of its victims are children.

Researchers believe that half a billion people carry malaria parasites. They got the parasites when an infected mosquito bit them. The disease may stay dormant for months before the person gets sick.

There are drugs to treat malaria. But the parasites that cause malaria often become resistant to the drugs over time. So researchers must constantly look for new malaria drugs.

Malaria can be ➲ prevented by avoiding mosquito bites. In some places, people sleep under netting so that mosquitoes can't bite them.

🎧 Opening more medical clinics, like this one in Iraq, can improve health care.

Simple Cures

Developing drugs and vaccines takes a lot of time and money. Thankfully, some illnesses can be cured with simple, inexpensive treatments.

Unclean drinking water is a problem in many places. More than a billion of the world's people do not have access to clean drinking water. When children drink dirty water, they often get severe diarrhea. This can dangerously dehydrate an infant or small child.

Researchers came up with a simple treatment. They have children drink packets of water mixed with salts. The salts help the body retain water so the children do not become dehydrated. This simple treatment prevents a million deaths a year.

Conclusion

Medical researchers, doctors, and other scientists continue to work toward cures for many diseases. Some of the diseases that are most difficult to cure are also the most common.

You've probably had influenza, or the flu. The flu is easy to catch. It spreads through the air when someone coughs or sneezes. Having the flu is no fun, but it isn't usually dangerous. However, about 36,000 Americans die from the flu each year. The very old, very young, and people sick with other diseases can be killed by the flu.

Many people get a flu vaccine each year. But the flu is caused by an ever-changing virus. New strains of the flu show up all the time. This means that researchers must constantly collect new flu samples to make updated vaccines. It's an ongoing battle.

Deadly Flu

Some strains of the flu are more dangerous than others. In 1918–1919, a deadly strain of flu sped around the world. The Spanish flu pandemic killed 20 million people.

Ⓒ Scientists grow flu vaccine in chicken eggs.

Wormwood

The Chinese have been treating malarial fevers with an herb called wormwood for more than a thousand years. When scientists studied wormwood, they found a compound in the herb's leaves that kills malaria parasites in the blood. The compound is now used in drugs to cure malaria.

Medical researchers have scoured the globe in search of new cures for diseases. They do research on rainforest plants and sea creatures to see if they contain useful drugs.

Scientists also use powerful tools to study microbes up close. They even study the genes of bacteria and viruses. What they learn may someday help save millions of lives. One of those lives might even be yours.

⊙ Some plants kill disease-causing microbes. Researchers collect plants in the rain forest to see if they can be made into new drugs.

Glossary

antibiotic *(an-tee-bigh-OT-ik)* a drug that kills bacteria *(page 10)*

bacteria *(bak-TEER-ee-uh)* single-celled microorganisms, some of which cause disease *(page 6)*

cell *(SEL)* the smallest working unit within an organism *(page 7)*

dissection *(digh-SEK-shuhn)* the thorough examination of an organism by cutting it open and studying its parts *(page 4)*

immune system *(i-MYEWN SIS-tum)* the body's way of fighting disease *(page 11)*

microbe *(MIGH-krohb)* a microscopic living organism *(page 5)*

mold *(MOHLD)* fungus that grows on food and damp surfaces *(page 9)*

pandemic *(pan-DEHM-ik)* a worldwide outbreak of disease *(page 17)*

pathogen *(PATH-uh-jen)* something that causes disease, such as viruses, bacteria, or parasites *(page 8)*

penicillin *(pen-uh-SIL-uhn)* a drug that kills some kinds of bacteria *(page 9)*

specimen *(SPES-uh-muhn)* something that is collected so it can be studied *(page 5)*

vaccine *(vak-SEEN)* a medicine that prevents a person from getting a certain disease *(page 11)*

virus *(VIGH-ruhs)* a very tiny and simple microbe that can cause disease; polio, measles, and the common cold are caused by viruses *(page 7)*

Index

Comprehension Check

Summarize

Use the Sequence Chart to summarize some of the big discoveries and events in medicine discussed in this book.

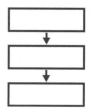

Think and Compare

1. Turn to page 5. What year were microbes discovered? What discoveries came afterward? *(Sequence)*

2. Did reading this book make you more concerned about diseases? Why? *(Evaluate)*

3. The law requires people who work in restaurants to wash their hands. This helps keep them from spreading germs to customers. Name some other ways that diseases are spread. What is done to prevent them from spreading? *(Analyze/Apply)*